inventions

WHAT?

WHAT IS THE SMALLEST ROBOT CALLED?

Om KIDZ
An imprint of Om Books International

WHAT?

CONTENTS

1 What is an invention?

An invention is the embodiment of a new idea in the form of a device or a process that aims at solving a specific problem. It also needs to be proven workable. A new invention can be patented, making its commercial use profitable.

Pocket fact

It's mine! When someone invents something, it needs to be patented. A patent is a right that lies with the owner of an invention. It prevents others from copying, using, selling or importing the invention without the inventor's permission.

2 What does an inventor do?

An inventor is a person who identifies problems and concentrates on ways to solve those problems. Inventors formulate ideas, methods, and processes and often design technical devices which usually make life better for human beings.

Find out!

If two people invent something together, who gets the patent?

Find out!

When was the unicycle invented?

3 What was the first wheel made of?

The first wheel was probably made of wood. Archaeological evidence suggests that the wheel was first used in Mesopotamia for pottery. The oldest wooden wheel discovered was found in Ljubljana, Slovenia, and is believed to date back to around 3200 BCE. Wheels started being used for transportation much later.

Pocket fact

John Kemp Starley, an English inventor and industrialist, invented the first modern bicycle in 1885.

4 What was the first bicycle called?

The Dandy Horse! The first human means of transport that used only two wheels in tandem, was invented by the German inventor Baron Karl von Drais. It was made of a wooden frame supported by two in-line wheels. The rider sat on the wooden frame with one leg on each side and pushed the vehicle with his or her feet while steering the front wheel. The Dandy Horse was introduced to the public in Mannheim, in 1817, and in Paris, in 1818. Also called 'Draisine' or 'Laufmaschine', this vehicle was the forerunner of the modern bicycle.

Find out!

Why do tyres have valve caps?

5 What was the first car like?

It was a two-seater vehicle with a four-stroke engine! The first car was invented by Carl Benz in 1885. The main features of this two-seater vehicle included-its high-speed fourstroke engine installed horizontally at the rear, the tubular steel frame, three wire-spoked wheels and the differential. It also had a controlled exhaust valve, an automatic intake slide, water/thermo electrical vibrator, and ignition with spark plug.

Pocket fact

A car has about 30,000 parts, counting every part down to the smallest screw. Some of these parts are made by the car manufacturing company while some are made by other suppliers.

6 What is a tyre made of?

A tyre is a covering for a wheel and it is usually made of rubber. It is ring-shaped and covers the rim of a wheel. Tyres used to be solid, but now only inflated tyres are used because they provide a cushioning for the wheel to absorb shocks when moving over rough terrain.

Find out!

Why do shirts have collars?

7 What was the earliest clothing made of?

Animal skin! Humans have been wearing clothes since hundreds of thousands of years. The earliest clothing was probably made of animal skin. It is assumed that humans have been wearing clothes since the last part of the Ice Age because it would have been impossible to survive without clothing at that point.

8 What does the 'T' in a T-shirt stand for?

The 'T' in a T-shirt is usually attributed to the T-shape of the garment when laid out. This theory is also supported by the existence of A-shirts (which are also called tank tops). T-shirt is also often seen as the abbreviation for Training Shirt.

Pocket fact

The necktie first originated in the 17th century in France. King Louis XIII hired Croatian mercenaries during a war, who wore a piece of cloth called 'sravat' around their neck as part of their uniform.

Find out!

Why does every new clock show the time 10:10?

9 What did people use to keep track of time before clocks?

Objects in the sky and some devices! The first mechanical clocks started appearing in the 13th and 14th centuries. Until then, people kept track of time by looking at the Sun, stars and the seasons of the year. Eventually, devices such as the sundial, obelisk, hourglass, clypsendra (based on the controlled flow of a liquid), candle clock and incense clock were invented to keep track of time.

Pocket fact

The oldest clock! The oldest clock in the world is located in Salisbury, England. It was created in 1386.

10 What is a smart watch?

A smart watch is a device that is equipped to do much more than just tell the time. The scope of functions for a smart watch depends on the variety that is used, but they are usually most effective when synced to a smart phone. Smart watches can do a lot but they cannot be as good as smart phones.

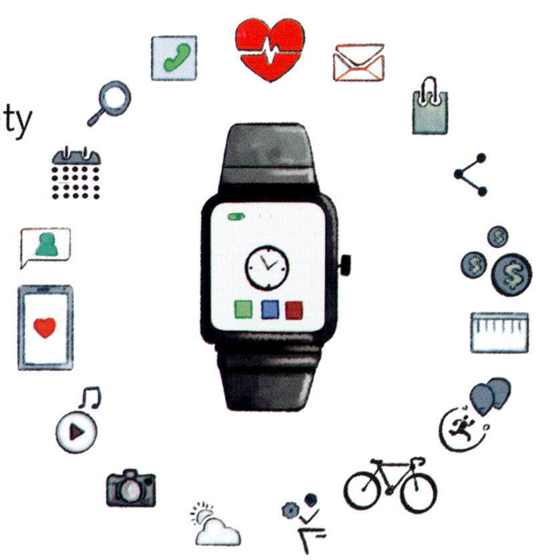

11 What is the history of shoes?

It dates backs to 1600-1200 BCE! Shoes have been used to shield the feet since ages. The earliest shoes were soft, made from wraparound leather, and resembled either sandals or moccasins. Then came rock sandals, leather shoes and sandals. In the 18th century, fabric shoes like the silk pair were considered very fashionable.

Pocket fact

Breaking in a new pair of shoes was not as easy as it is today. The earliest shoes were made on absolutely straight lasts. There was no difference between the right and the left shoe until 1850.

12 What is an aglet used for?

To keep the fibre of the shoelace from unravelling! An aglet is the hard metal or plastic coating present at the end of the shoelace, to prevent the fabric of the shoestrings from getting frayed. It also helps in putting the shoelaces through the eyelets of the shoes. Today, most of the aglets are made by wrapping the end of the shoelaces with plastic coating.

Find out!

When was the ice cream cone invented and by whom?

13 What was the first chocolate like?

It was a beverage made from the cacao bean! Chocolate history begins in Mesoamerica in 1900 BCE. The Maya, Toltec, and Aztec people cultivated the cacao tree more than 3,000 years ago. However, the first people to use chocolate as a beverage were probably the Olmec of, what is today, southeast Mexico. The Mayans also used chocolate in religious rituals but it was strictly for drinking purposes. Chocolate came to be used in solid form only in the 1850s.

Pocket fact

The first chocolate bar was made in 1842 by the British chocolate company called Cadbury.

14 What were the ingredients of the first ice cream?

Just ice and honey or fruits! There is no specific record of when or who invented ice cream but this cold dessert has been known to date back to the 2nd century BCE. We know that Alexander the Great enjoyed having snow or ice flavoured with honey. Also, during the Roman Empire, Nero Claudius Caesar (CE 54–86) was known to send runners to fetch snow from the mountains so that he could have it with fruits and juices.

Find out!

In which year was iced tea invented and by whom?

15 What is the difference between tomato sauce and tomato ketchup?

The difference between tomato sauce and tomato ketchup lies in its preparation! In the United States, tomatoes, sugar, vinegar and spices are used to make ketchup and as a rule, it is always served cold. Sauces involve the use of tomatoes, oil, meat or vegetable and spices. Vinegar is not used. Also, sauces are generally served hot.

Pocket fact

Ketchup bottles were not always upside down. A shop owner named Paul Brown in Mich designed a new storable upside down bottle so that it could open easily when squeezed and shut securely. It earned Paul Brown $13 million.

16 What is the history of tea?

The history of tea dates back to around 2700 BCE in China. Most sources also trace the origin of the tea plant to Tibet and northern India. Tea was used as a medicinal beverage for a thousand years. It was obtained by boiling fresh leaves in water. The popularity of tea grew around the 3rd century CE when tea cultivation and processing began and it soon became a daily drink.

WHAT?

Find out!

How many parts does a coin have?
Can you name them?

17 What was the mode of sale and purchase before the invention of currency?

The barter system! The medium of exchange before the invention of currency was barter, a system where transaction took place through the exchange of goods and services. It was slow and inconvenient because people had to find other people with whom they could make deals where both parties were satisfied. The barter system was slowly made easier by the exchange of easily tradable goods like salt, weapons and animal skins.

18 What led to the invention of the dollar sign?

The origin of the dollar sign is shrouded in mystery but the most commonly accepted theory that comes from the Bureau of Engraving and Printing is that the Spanish Peso, which was the basic currency of Spanish America, was abbreviated as PS. It is believed that the two alphabets merged together to lead to the formation of the US dollar sign. The sign first appeared in the 1800s and was already widely used by the time the American paper dollar was printed in 1875.

Pocket fact

Piggy bank! The term 'piggy bank' was derived from the word 'pygg'. In Old English, pygg was a type of clay that was used to make jars and dishes that held money.

Find out!

What is the meaning of the word Sudoku?

19 What is the history of Sudoku?

The name comes from Japan but the puzzle comes from Switzerland! Sudoku has its roots in ancient magic squares or number puzzles. In 1783, a Swiss mathematician named Leonhard Euler, devised 'Latin Squares' and called it 'a new kind of magic squares'. It was a grid in which each number was repeated only once in each row or column. The modern Sudoku was first introduced by Howard Garnes in the American Dell magazine, New York in 1979. The difference was that the grids were subdivided into blocks of nine of 3x3 squares.

Pocket fact

Who gave the term robot?
The word 'robot' was first used by Czech playwright Karel Capek in his play RUR, Rossum's Universal Robots in 1921. The play was about the destruction of humanity by robots.

20 What is the smallest robot called?

It's called the RoboBee! The world's smallest robot was developed by a research team at Harvard University in 2009. RoboBee was modelled on an insect and is the smallest man-made device with a wingspan of 3 centimetres. The RoboBee project was launched to make a fully autonomous swarm of flying robots for applications such as search and rescue and artificial pollination.

Find out!

The @ sign is commonly known as 'at' sign or symbol. What is it actually called?

21 What is an e-mail ID?

E-mail ID is just another name for e-mail address. Electronic mail (e-mail) is a method of exchanging messages between people using the electronic medium. E-mails can operate across computer networks, that is, the Internet. To send and receive e-mails, you should have an e-mail ID. It's just like your address in a locality. The default format of an e-mail ID is Username@domain.com. You can modify the part before the @ sign. But the domain name cannot be modified.

Pocket fact

E-mail from space! E-mails cannot only travel around the world but they can also be sent from space. The first e-mail from space was sent in 1991 by the crew of STS-43 Atlantis. They used Apple's AppleLink software on a Macintosh Portable to send an e-mail.

22 What amount of time does an e-mail take to reach us?

It takes just a few seconds! Usually e-mails are delivered instantly (within seconds) to the recipients. But the exact speed of the e-mail depends upon factors such as Internet traffic and server load at particular times of the day. In general, however, e-mail delivery can be almost instantaneous under best conditions. If you have a good internet speed, you can send an e-mail to a friend halfway around the world, which they will receive within seconds of your sending it!

Find out!

What's the difference between 3D and 5D movies?

23 What is a 3D movie?

A 3D movie refers to a three-dimensional film. Dimensions are extensions in a particular direction. For example, the two-dimensional (2D) images have two dimensions: length and width, while the 3D images have length, width and depth. When you watch a 2D movie, the visual effect is similar to that of a drawing on the paper. In 3D movies, you see a slightly different picture like cars flying towards you or snowflakes floating in the air around you. The 3D effect is experienced in the real world by wearing special glasses which create two different images, so each eye has its own slightly different view. The brain then puts the two images together to form one 3D image that has depth to it.

Pocket fact

The first viewing device that combines two pictures in one, a forerunner of the 3D image was invented by William Friese Greene of UK in 1894.

24 What was the first 3D movie called?

It was called *The Power of Love!* The first 3D movie shown to an out-of-house audience was *The Power of Love*, which was premiered at the Ambassador Hotel Theater in Los Angeles on 27 September 1922. This movie used the dual-strip projection and was projected in the red/green anaglyph format. Anaglyph format refers to the 3D effect that is achieved by encoding each eye's image using filters of different colours, typically red and cyan.

Find out!

When was the first mobile phone call made?

25 What is a mobile network?

A mobile network refers to a radio network distributed over land through cells where each cell includes a fixed location transceiver known as base station. These cells work together to provide radio coverage over larger geographical areas. The network provides services to mobile phone users. These services include making voice and video calls, sending SMS (texts) and MMS messages (picture messages) and internet access.

Pocket fact

The first finger-driven touchscreen was invented by E.A. Johnson in 1965 at the Royal Radar Establishment in Malvern, United Kingdom.

26 What's so special about touchscreens?

It enables the user to interact directly with the display, rather than using a mouse! A touchscreen is an input and output device layered on the top of the electronic visual display of a cell phone or computer. One can give input or control the phone or computer functions through simple or multi-touch gestures, by just touching the screen with a special stylus and/or one or more fingers.

OTHER TITLES IN THIS SERIES